Lights, Camera, Action!

A Guide To Video Instruction and Production In The Classroom

By Bruce Limpus

Illustrations by Peggy Peters

Prufrock
Press Post Office Box 8813
Waco, Texas 76714-8813
1-800-998-2208

Acknowledgments

My thanks to San Antonio Youth Literacy for getting me started in video and supporting my classes for the last eight years. For the most part, the information in this book has been developed from my personal experience while working with video in the classroom, but I owe a great deal to the media professionals who gave their time and expertise to me and my students in many workshops and classroom visits. I also wish to express my thanks to the Edgewood Independent School District and Edgewood High School in particular for encouraging me to experiment as I teach; to my daughter, Teresa Zapp, for her valuable input on using video in the kindergarten classroom; to Ms. Peggy Peters who created some beautiful illustrations; and to Don and Mary Lou Hymel who helped with proofreading.

Table of Contents

Introduction
Performance Based Video Projects:
A Valuable Classroom Strategy

As teachers we are all looking for new teaching methods that will give the students a learning experience they will carry with them throughout their lives. We try everything—some things work and some don't—but no teacher worth the name is ever completely satisfied with his or her methods, and no single teaching strategy is the answer to the problem. Creating video productions in the classroom is not the complete and magic solution to the problems of education, but it is a good teaching method that works, and, in fact, will give the student a learning experience that he or she will never forget.

Seven years ago, my high school campus was approached by SAYL (San Antonio Youth Literacy) asking us how they could help us address the problem of functional illiteracy in the area. Since our school district is one of the poorest in the state of Texas serving an almost totally Hispanic population in an extremely economically depressed area, we were delighted to take advantage of any help we could get. After several meetings and much discussion, someone suggested that if SAYL could provide us with some video equipment, we might be able to do something new and interesting.

Given that one of the largest contributing factors to the poor academic achievement of our students is the lack of a positive self-image, and that probably the largest media influence on all recent generations of students is television, we felt that our video program had great possibilities. In San Antonio's west side, to "come out on TV" is considered success and recognition beyond imagination. If the students could see themselves is a successful mode and performing on a television screen, we might be making a step in the direction of enhancing the students' self-images. And, even more, it might be fun.

As the program progressed, we discovered that while the students were producing a television project, they were also working with most of the essential elements mandated in the state English curriculum. When the gifted and talented program was instituted on our campus, I soon discovered that video projects were ideal in challenging the diverse talents of the gifted students.

As I am primarily an English teacher with some experience in drama, I was given the project to develop; and, as expected, the possibilities inherent in video projects fit in well with much of the English curriculum. But as time went by, I discovered that video also works well with many other areas of study. It is, for example, particularly well suited for social studies and foreign language courses. Science classes can use the method for demonstrations and projects. Even math classes can use the "mini-teach" project to reinforce some special lesson.

It may be important to note that we teachers might be reluctant to try anything very creative with a video project because we feel insecure with the technical aspect of the equipment. I can only say that I had never held a video camera in my hands before I started using it in the classroom. Whatever skills I have, they have never included the technical manipulation of complicated equipment. I am, after all, an old English teacher. But when we received our first camera, it was like Christmas. The students, as if by magic, learned the nuances and details of the operation of the equipment instantly, and over the years have managed even to teach me something about it, too.

All of my experience has been in secondary education, but I know that video projects are also valuable in elementary classes. My daughter, who is an elementary teacher, usually produces one large video project a year with her students. I plan to share some of her experience in a later chapter.

When beginning a video program, I found it best to start with a small, simple project that will give the students an idea of what it takes to produce a video presentation. With these smaller projects, I divide their audience, decide on their specific project, write the script, and make a detailed production sheet which will include the actors, technical crew, location of shoot, and the shooting and editing schedule. I usually require the students to design a story board. Making a story board is similar to making a comic book with each panel showing the video composition of each shot. This gives the students a visual idea of what they want the video to look like.

Then comes the videotaping. You will probably find that a number of takes are required for each scene or shot. The forgotten line, the accident, the sudden attack of the tied tongue will slow down the process. But by far the biggest culprit in causing the takes to mount up is the giggles. It happens to them all, and it will sorely test your patience.

After the taping you will need to select music, record voice-overs, and edit the whole thing together. If you have editing equipment, this process is easier and will give you a more professional end-product. But you can put together good and exciting projects with just a camera, a television set, and a VCR.

What you end up with is a few minutes of a completed video project. If you have worked one class period a day, you will be lucky to complete a small project in a week. There is more than a week's work for a few minutes of product. But the students will love it and will want to watch it over and over again. What is even more important is that they will have discovered a medium that has enormous creative possibilities. Research, organization, writing, assimilation, speaking, art, and music all will have played a significant role in preparing the video production.

With that introduction, the students can move into more ambitious projects. I like to have the students generate the projects from the literature studied in the class, usually in the form of a drama. But the television commercial, the documentary, the news program, the mini-teach, the game show, and what is probably the most fun of all, the continuing soap opera, can all be satisfactory and very exciting projects for the students.

Publishing is almost as important as producing the project. To have validity, the video project must be seen by someone. If your school has some type of closed-circuit television system, such as Channel One, it is ideal for broadcasting your project. At times, we have set up a VCR and monitor in the cafeteria during lunch to air some of our projects. As you can imagine, the soap opera is very popular. Teachers can share tapes that are germane to the units they are teaching. We exchange tapes by mail with a school about 200 miles away so that we can show off our projects and also see what other people are doing. There are video competitions, and the possibility of public-access television. These projects are most gratifying to the students when they know that other people will see their talents in action.

All children, especially teenagers, are inordinately conscious and sensitive about who they are and how they appear to others. The prospect of seeing themselves (and being seen) for the first time on television can be extremely threatening. I make certain that only positive critical remarks are allowed when we are evaluating a project. Once the students see that they are doing at least as well as others, and that they don't look nearly as bad or absurd as they feared, they have come a long way in repairing negative self-concepts. And I have the pleasure of watching their confidence and self-awareness grow.

Besides being a method to make literature and history come alive, a method to air perplexing and controversial problems, and a vehicle addressing the organization, research, writing, speaking, and creative skills of the students, video production is fun. The students will look forward to participating in the class. As a teacher, you can't ask for any more than that.

PART I
Organizing and Producing the Video Project

Chapter 1
Equipment

Obtaining the equipment to produce video projects in your classroom may seem like a difficult and very expensive proposition, but this is not necessarily so. Of course you can buy a lot of expensive equipment if you have the funds, but all you really need is a video camera, a VCR, and a monitor. I would be surprised to hear about a school these days that does not have a TV set and a VCR available, and most schools will have a video camera in their audio/video rooms to loan out for projects. If your school does not have this rudimentary equipment, you need to promote their purchase with your principal. You might tactfully suggest that it is time for your school to join the 20th century.

Cameras

The camera is naturally the most essential piece of equipment because it provides the raw material for your production. A camcorder would be the best type of camera for your purposes. With a camcorder you have the option of using a battery or a wall plug for power.

The advantage of using a battery is that you can carry the camera outside or any other place where there is not a power source. It also gives you the freedom to move around as you are taping without being hampered by power lines. But a battery has only limited life until it must be recharged. One of the annoying little problems is finding that someone forgot to recharge the battery just when you are going out on a shoot. It could cause the loss of a valuable class period which had been planned for filming.

It is a good idea to use regular wall-plug power whenever possible to prolong the life of your battery. Often batteries cannot tolerate a lot of rough use on a daily basis, and you don't want to be buying new batteries regularly. There are a lot of different sizes and kinds of batteries. It is extremely important to follow your camcorder instructions exactly when it comes to recharging your battery.

If you are selecting a camera, choose one that is sturdy, without a lot of salient parts sticking out. Students are sometimes a bit clumsy and sometimes a bit thoughtless, so you want a minimum of parts that could break off easily. I teach a year-long visual media class that uses the camera daily. With this steady use, we feel lucky if a camera lasts two years.

The eight millimeter camera is very popular for home video. It is much smaller, and therefore, a good deal lighter to carry around. It uses a small eight millimeter tape that is about the size of an audio tape. You must connect the camera to the VCR to play on the video screen and to copy to a regular VHS tape. (Some systems provide a cassette into which you insert the eight millimeter tape to enable you to play it in a VCR.)

I have found that the video quality of these small cameras is excellent, often better than the regular camcorder. But even though I have had some success with using this type of camera in the classroom (it was the only kind of camera that I had available at the time), I would not recommend it. The controls are tiny and too delicate for the often clumsy treatment that untrained students can give it.

Some cameras can be adjusted to record at different speeds. The three speeds that are usually featured are SP, LP, and EP/SLP. Many people will immediately use EP/SLP because you can get a run of 360 minutes on one tape. But that type of tape economy is not worth the difference in the quality that you would get at a faster speed. SP, which will give you a run of 120 minutes on the tape, is the recommended speed for high quality video recording.

Cameras come with various options that could be helpful: manual or automatic focus, fade, indoor/outdoor automatic shutter adjust, back light, and zoom lens. Some cameras can be equipped with a character generator that will allow you to make titles and graphics, and some with small light attachments for situations when light is needed.

VCR and Monitor

You will need a good VCR not only for play-back but also for editing. It would be helpful if you have a VCR that allows you to dub audio without altering the video. This capability allows you to make voice-overs and add music or sound effects to your project.

Whether a tape has been recorded at SP, LP, or EP/SLP, most VCRs manufactured for home use will play back automatically at the recorded speed for viewing on the monitor. When copying a tape on a VCR you have the option of making the copy at one of these speeds. However, the VCRs on many large editing banks operate only at SP with the understanding, I suppose, that most people realize that SP gives the best quality.

The VCR connected with the monitor (TV set) allows you to see what the picture will be on the tape while you are recording it. Most of the time the view finder on the camera does not give you a completely accurate image of what actually will be recorded on the tape with respect to composition and color. Running the camera through the VCR to the monitor allows you to use the image on the TV set as your view finder, and you can make sure that your camera is focused where it should be.

Editing

Basic editing techniques are simpler than they may seem using these three components—camera, VCR, and monitor:
1. Attach jacks to the "audio out" and "video out" jack plugs in your camera or power pack.
2. Attach the other end of these jacks into the "audio in" and "video in" jack plugs on your VCR.
3. Insert the video cassette with your taped material into the camera.
4. Insert a blank cassette into the VCR.
5. Put the VCR on "play" and "record" at the same time, then hit the pause button on your remote controller.
6. Put your camera in the play-back mode and cue up the picture to be edited, then hit "play."

7.   Using the "pause" button on the VCR remote con-
     troller, you can record what you want by turning the
     "pause" button on and off. This will give you good edits
     without significant glitches.

It is important not to hit "stop" on your VCR while you
are editing, because it will give you a rather large glitch.
Also some VCRs will turn off after a certain period of time
while it is in the "pause" mode, so it is necessary to study
your raw tape and plan exactly your editing plan so that
you can edit quickly and cleanly.

You can accomplish a certain amount of editing while
actually taping by shooting scenes in sequence and going
back and recording over the out-takes. This makes final editing a lot easier. Be sure that when you are shooting to give a
count of five after you have turned on the "record" button on
your camera before the action begins. Also give a count of five
at the end of each take before you turn the "record" button to
the off position. This will save you missing a bit at the beginning and the end of your take. Remember: **If it is not on the
tape, it is gone forever!** No amount of creative editing can
replace words or actions that are missing on the tape.

Some "Nice-to-have" Equipment

The Tripod

While I am categorizing the tripod as a piece of "nice-
to-have equipment," it is, however, extremely useful, and I
would recommend that you get one somehow before you
start your production. Attaching your camera to a tripod
will eliminate camera movement while taping, and assure
that the camera is in exactly the same position from one
take to another. As long as the actors are always on their
marks, camera continuity can be maintained.

Cameras are often heavy, and long sessions of taping can
be exhausting to your camera operator. The tripod can relieve
that problem. If you are selecting a tripod for purchase, you
need to choose one that is sturdy enough to maintain the
weight of the camera. It has been my experience that tripods
have a shorter life than cameras, so it is important to find one
that has good, strong knobs for its functions.

Lighting

Ordinary incandescent or fluorescent lighting is not very good for video lighting. I have tried setting up cheap lighting with big scoop lights that I bought in the hardware store, but I found that even though these items give enough light, they wash out the color. This can be a problem when you are trying to shoot a dark scene with deep shadows. If you need to address this problem, you can purchase a rudimentary photographic lighting kit at a fairly reasonable price. Also, some cameras have a small light attachment available.

The Dolly

A dolly is nice-to-have, but not absolutely necessary. A dolly is a type of platform on wheels that will hold a tripod. This piece of equipment will allow you to move the camera steadily and exactly. For example, if you want to follow the actor's movement down the hall, you can push the camera, tripod and all, along with the actor in a perfectly smooth movement.

The Editing Bank

Of course an editing bank is really nice to have. It consists of two VCRs, two monitors, and a control panel. This equipment allows you to edit from one tape to another quickly, accurately, and easily. The functions of the control panel range from simple editing to special effects, sound mixing, automatic fade, character generating, etc. Unfortunately these set-ups are quite expensive, depending on the amount of sophisticated functions that they offer. Some school districts will have this equipment at some central location available for your use, and if they do they probably will have someone to teach you how to use it and to help you with it. (I have noticed that local TV stations will often be very helpful in this respect if they are approached in the right way.)

It is possible to find various items of equipment on the market that will give you some limited editing functions you can use with your basic camera-VCR-TV equipment to enhance your editing. There is, for example, a rather inexpensive "mini-editor" that will give you an automatic fade-in and fade-out capability as you edit. It will also allow you to mix music or sound from one or two external sources such as audio recorders.

Some of these "mini-editors" also have a function called a "video enhancer." Once you have a master tape that has been completely edited to your satisfaction, it is necessary to make all copies from the original master or the copies will degenerate. Copies from copies from copies gradually degenerate until they become so distorted that they are useless. The master copy is, in fact, the second generation. (The first generation would be the raw takes.) The video enhancer can sometimes make up for a bit of this distortion.

Microphones

All video cameras sold for home use are equipped with a built-in microphone. This is generally sufficient for most classroom use. Once you learn the limitations of the microphone that is provided, you can prepare for them. If you hold the camera too far away from actors, the dialogue can be lost. If you are trying to record a conversation in a busy school hallway between classes, the noise will drown out the conversation. If you are shooting outside, the slightest breeze can sound like a wind of gale force when you play it back. Experimenting and knowing what to expect will help you to overcome some of these problems.

Sound quality can be an on-going problem, and, if you can afford it, external microphone systems can solve them. The shot-gun microphone, for instance, will allow you to record sound at a distance. These microphones run from cheap to very expensive, depending, naturally, on the quality of the equipment.

Hand-held microphones can be very useful in interviews or other situations where the presence of the microphone does not distract from the intent of the production. This requires a cable from the microphone to the camera. If you need to use more than one microphone, then you must have a mixer that will mix the sound of both microphones into the camera. You can also hide microphones on the set where they can pick up the sound and not be seen. Lavaliere microphones are very small and can be hidden and attached to the actor's clothing. These microphones work well and are especially suited for the interview situation.

Audio Tape Recorder

You will probably need to have access to an audio tape recorder to help you produce the sound for your production. We use a cassette recorder and collect the music and sound effects that we will need. The recorder should have a microphone for the recording of various sounds. Certain students can find a genuine creative outlet in discovering inventive ways to create needed sounds. It is wise to collect sounds and maintain a sound effect library. I often find a couple of students who love this aspect of television production, and I give them the title of "foley," which is the film industry's name for those responsible for sound effects.

New Developments

New equipment with new functions is being developed every day. Since I have been working with video, I have seen all kinds of new developments in equipment, and prices become more reasonable on equipment that once cost too much to consider. As time goes on, more sophistication in your video productions will be possible.

But, again, if you have only a camera, a VCR, and a monitor, you can still create a valuable learning experience for your students.

Chapter 2
Pre-production Planning

"Do we really need to do all of this writing?" That is the plaintive cry of the students who want to get out the camera and start shooting, making it up as they go. That approach has some limited merit in respect to finding a way of looking at the world and trying to put it together later. But as in all artistic endeavors, the quality of the product depends a great deal on the amount of good planning that is done.

Working in Teams

The students need to learn to work in teams creatively and efficiently. This can be introduced with group exercises. Divide the students into small groups of four or five. Each group must select a leader, whose responsibility is to keep everyone in the group involved and keep the group on task; a recorder, whose responsibility it is to write down and record everything that the team resolves; and a reporter, who will report the product of the team's effort to the class.

Present the teams with a hypothetical task to perform.

Example: "The class has been offered $500 for new equipment or materials if the need can be justified. The team must present its recommendation with valid reasons for its choice."

Give the teams 15 to 20 minutes to prepare their report, and then have each present its recommendations to the class. You can be as creative as you like in coming up with hypothetical problems and tasks. This will give the students training in working in groups and a model to follow when they need to make use of group dynamics.

Planning and Brainstorming

The ideal situation is one where the students, not the teacher, do the planning. Planning may constitute more than 50 percent of the learning process, and all students need to explore ideas and find ways to organize them. The teacher, of course, guides and assists in this process. It is okay for the teacher to suggest ideas, too, but most of this work should be done by the students.

Generally, the place to start is brainstorming. This is a good beginning technique that works whether the project is a news broadcast, a documentary, a drama, etc. The technique of brainstorming is to throw out the problem and allow the students to make suggestions off the tops of their heads. It is a good idea to encourage the students to express whatever comes into their minds. The recorder should write down all the suggestions no matter how silly they may sound. Sometimes the silliest, most off-the-wall ideas become the freshest and the most workable. After that the students will have a good deal of material with which they can organize a workable plan.

The Script

Next the script needs to be written. Some students may find it easy to go straight to the script format and start writing, but most will need to start by writing out a narrative of the action. This can be a preparatory step to rounding out the action and can aid the students in focusing in on developing scenes. But eventually a shooting script must be written.

An individual student can prepare the script, or a team of writers can be assigned to work together. You can decide this by determining the way your students work best. I have had students who feel they must work alone, and they have often produced brilliant work. But for most students, being a member of a team allows them to feed off each other when they are working on a script project. They get more input, and they feel more secure.

The format of a television script is simply a sheet of paper with a vertical line down the middle. One side of the line is for audio, and the other side is for video.

On the audio side, everything is written out in the sequence in which it will be heard on the final tape. This includes music, dialogue, sound effects, and voice-overs.

On the video side, everything is written out in the sequence that will be seen on the final tape. The video side of the script must correspond to the audio side. For instance, on the video side it might say, "A student sitting at a desk, taking a test, holding his or her head and looking confused." Then across to the audio side directly corresponding to this, it might say, "(Voice over) Do tests give you a headache?" This will allow the director and the camera operator to plan the filming of each shot. It will also give the actors a script to study for their lines.

The Story Board

The story board is also a useful device for organizing a video production. The story board is a series of rectangles drawn in the shape of television screens. Each rectangle represents a camera shot. It will look somewhat like a cartoon strip when it is finished. The idea is to have a plan of each camera angle or each different shot. It is not necessary to be a skilled artist to draw the necessary pictures in the story board; simple stick figures and rudimentary drawing will put the idea across.

With the story board you can organize the shooting so that there will be a variety of shots (close-up, two-shot, wide-angle, etc.). This will make your production more interesting to watch and give it a more professional look. In addition, it will save you a lot of time when it comes to the actual shooting.

It is possible to buy pads of prepared blank story board sheets, but it is a simple matter to make your own with a ruler and a pencil. A sample page of blank story board rectangles can be photocopied and distributed to the students for use.

Developing a Production Sheet

In the real, live world of television production, budget unfortunately can become more important than artistic value. If schedules are not met, the cost of a production can get out of hand. The expression, "time is money," has real meaning in a production studio. In the classroom we are not that concerned with actual money; but time itself is valuable, even precious. Most schools allot less than an hour per class, and some class periods are as short as 45 minutes. By the time the equipment is set up, the set is arranged, and the actors are in costume and make-up, it doesn't leave much time for shooting. Then of course you have to arrange for time to put the equipment away, and to let your actors change back into their school clothes before the bell rings. This makes scheduling and planning doubly important.

Developing a production sheet will help the students plan in detail so that the shooting will run smoothly. It will list who the director and assistant director will be. (With students who have had no experience with video, it is sometimes a good idea for the teacher to be the director.) All personnel involved in the production should be listed, including the camera operator, the actors, the students who are responsible for script, story board, props, sets, costumes, make-up, lights, editing, etc. This list will be the guide for creating the credits at the end of the production.

You then need to organize a pre-production schedule. This will show projected deadlines for the completion of the set, costumes, props, sound effects, etc. Sometimes it is necessary to arrange for shooting locations other than the classroom, and perhaps permission must be obtained for their use. Everything should be arranged and ready when it comes time to shoot.

The shooting schedule is very important. This will indicate what parts of the script will be shot on which days. With a good shooting schedule, the students can be prepared quickly for the day's shooting. If you have more than one group planning and working on different productions, the shooting schedule can be of enormous importance. Unless you want complete chaos, a firm schedule must be maintained.

Production Meeting

I have had as many as four groups working on different projects in various stages of production development at the same time. With two cameras, one classroom, and, of course, only one teacher to supervise, everything has to be organized carefully. Under these conditions I conduct a production meeting of all the students every Friday. In that meeting each group reports on its progress. Then we adjust and firm up the schedule for the following week. This enables us to have some flexibility according to the needs of each group.

When working with high school students, it is necessary to establish a certain amount of trust and responsibility with the students. Usually, good leaders are easily identified and are willing to come forward. If I have two groups working in the classroom and two groups shooting at different locations, I have to trust somebody because I can't be in more than one place at a time. Over the years I have had very few problems in this respect.

Even though some students will be impatient with the planning stage of the production and will be eager to get the camera in their hands and start making a television show, they should learn the value of pre-production planning. At times it may be necessary to alter your plans as you go along (the best laid plans of mice and men ...), but you will find that the more completely you plan, the smoother your production will be.

Chapter 3
Getting Started

One of the amazing things about producing a video is that you don't really need a lot of space. If you stay away from wide-angle shots, you can give the impression of many varied locations by leaving to the imagination of the audience everything that is not in the picture. Simply suggest that you are on the top of the Empire State Building or in a dungeon beneath the castle.

Naturally it would be nice to have a room all your own that you could turn into a sound stage, but few teachers have that option. However, with a little ingenuity, you can create a studio in a corner of your classroom that will function satisfactorily for shooting scenes; and, what is more, it can be arranged so that it will not interfere too greatly with your other classes.

I suggest a corner, because more can be done with that kind of an angle and the light can be controlled better. You will then need something to support whatever is required to suggest the scene. Since I am located in a high school, I frequently call on the woodworking department to construct items for my sets. A volunteer parent who is good at carpentry can be of great help. And, of course, the students themselves can do whatever building is necessary.

Using Folding Flats

I have found that screens similar to folding flats used on the stage are perfect for video use. These are simply a couple of wooden frames attached together with hinges and covered with muslin or some other fairly heavy cloth. The flats should be from seven to eight feet high so that your tallest student can stand in front of it without his or her head above the top of the flat.

You can fit the folding flat into a corner and turn it into anything you like. It could be a forest or a living room with pictures on the wall. I use different colors of cloth to fasten onto the flat depending on what is needed for the scene. The flat can support butcher paper or cardboard on which the students have painted scenery. Across the top of the angled flat, I sometimes fasten a board from which I can hang things such as microphones or special lighting or even a floating trumpet for a seance scene. With some imagination, a great deal can be done with a set-up such as this. When the folding flats are not in use, they can be folded up and stored out of the way until they are needed again.

Many of the projects that my students have produced have been taped totally in the corner of my room. This was the case of the "Mummy's Curse" (a project that I have outlined in another chapter). An Egyptian tomb was needed, and there were only two sets necessary. I asked the custodians to save the cardboard cartons that come into the school for me, and we made the entrance to the tomb out of this cardboard all painted to look like stones. Inside the tomb, we covered the flats with cardboard and painted them with colorful Egyptian wall paintings and hieroglyphics.

We set up two folding flats to enclose the area on three sides. The area was small but with clever blocking and organization it worked very well.

Making and Collecting Props

Most of the props that you need can be collected from the students, who will bring those items from home. Toys often make good props, like weapons or special equipment for specific careers, such a medical, police, etc. You might be surprised at what the students will come up with. We were working on a play that took place during the Vietnam War, and the actors came with an arsenal of plastic weapons, walkie-talkies, and camouflage uniforms.

There will be times that you need to manufacture certain prop items. Papier-maché, cardboard, wood, plastic, and paint can all be used. The results will vary according to the creativity of your students. Often it is not necessary to be absolutely exact when you are making a prop, because a simple suggestion can look genuine on camera. We made a monkey's paw out of painted cardboard, and when you looked at it, it looked just like painted cardboard. But used in the scene on tape, it looked genuine.

Example of a Video Script Prepared by
High School Students
(Vita-Brain Commercial)

Video	Audio
Student sitting at desk taking test. (1 shot) (1)	Music lead in.
Reacts confused. (2)	Voice over: What was the shoe size of Calvin Coolidge?
Scratches head. (3)	VO: What is the converse valence of the true strellis on the grisnovith of the framistan?
Nods and holds head? (4)	VO: Do tests give you a headache?
Claps hands on ears. (5)	VO: Do you sometimes feel your brains leading out of your ears?
(Cut to announcer holding a bottle of pills) 1 shot (6)	VO: Then try Vita-Brain, the smart pill that will help you through any test crisis.
Close up on pills grouped by colors. Finger points out each color. (7)	VO: Red for English, Green for sciences, Yellow for social studies, Orange for math.
(Cut to student) Taking pill. (8)	VO: Just take the correct pill for each tough question.
Student smiles and recites (9)	Student: Four score and seven years ago our ...
Student begins to write (10)	VO: Vita-Brain for your GPA. Warning. A double dose is required for freshmen.
Fade to black.	Music to fade.

Example of a Production Sheet

PROJECT TITLE: Vita-Brain (commercial)
PROJECTED AUDIENCE: Students
DIRECTOR: Alfred Ramirez
ASSISTANT DIRECTOR: Gloria Munoz
CAMERA: Robert Torres
PROPS, SET, MAKE-UP: Beatrice Luna
CAST: David Hernandez (student)
      Abel Noriega (Announcer and voice over)
SCRIPT: Beatrice Luna
STORY BOARD: Robert Torres
LIGHTS: Beatrice Luna
EDITING: Alfred Ramirez
      Gloria Munoz
SOUND: Abel Noriega

PROPERTY LIST
1. Pill bottle
2. M and Ms (to be used as pills)
3. Notebook paper
4. Pencil
5. School Desk

COSTUMES
1. Boy's dress with tee shirt. (Student)
2. Adult man's dress, white shirt, tie, glasses (Announcer)

SHOOTING LOCATION
All shots in school classroom.

PROJECTED SCHEDULE
Two days taping.
Two days editing.
One day re-shoot.

Shooting on Location

Some scenes will require shooting at a location other than in your room. Often these locations are readily available, and it is much more efficient to use them than to try to fake it in your room studio. In the Vietnam play that I have mentioned, we found a small wooded area close to the campus, and with about an hour and a half of shooting, we were able to get ample footage of soldiers on patrol, breaking through foliage, etc., to give our production an authentic look.

On any high school campus there are many varied locations that can be used. There is the gymnasium, the different shops, the teachers' lounge, offices, the cafeteria, and interesting classrooms. The home economics department usually has a kitchen and sometimes models of dining rooms and bathrooms. Of course if your play is set in a school, you can shoot the entire production in an authentic location.

Students love to go out and shoot on location. For one thing, they like to get out of the classroom for a while. But what is more important, they like to be seen by others doing their projects. It makes them feel special, and can go a long way to establish positive self-images.

Using the Camera

The person operating the camera is responsible for a good deal more than turning the camera on when the director says "rolling" and turning it off when the director says "cut." It is up to the camera operator to make sure that the focus is correct, the composition of the picture is good, and any zooming or panning is graceful and appropriate. Perhaps the most important responsibility of the camera operator is to make sure that the scene being shot has a good leader at the beginning and at least a five second run at the end of the take.

Keeping the Camera Steady

One of the unfortunate earmarks of home video is the jiggling of the camera and the earthquake jumping of the picture. This can ruin a video, but it can be overcome by using a tripod. The tripod will hold the camera steady, and will allow you to move the camera vertically and horizontally in smooth, easy motions. You should always use a tripod when possible.

But the camera operator should learn hand-held camera techniques without a tripod, because there are going to be occasions when a tripod is not available or practical. The camera rests on the shoulder with one hand holding the camera steady and the other controlling the record button and the zoom. It takes a great deal of skill and stamina to hold completely still while you are taping, but this is what is required if you do not have a tripod. Using a hand held camera can be very tiring in long sessions.

The Zoom

The students generally want to zoom in and out on every shot; therefore, the first thing you should do is to try to discourage the students' love affair with the zoom control. The zoom is very useful in that it allows you to go from a long shot to a close-up gradually in one take, and vice-versa. But it should be used very sparingly, and it should be planned. In a comparatively long project such as "The Curse of the Mummy" (a project outlined in another chapter) there are only three shots when the zoom control is used.

The Pan Shot

The same applies to panning. Panning is moving the camera vertically or horizontally in the same take. You should pan the camera slowly and smoothly so that the details of the scene are clearly in view. Beginners often pan too quickly producing a dizzying effect. This dizzying "spray-the-garden" shot can be a good special effect if that is what you want. Panning should be used sparingly.

The Follow Shot and Dolly

A follow shot is when the camera follows some movement in the scene. For example, if the actor in the scene walks from the desk to the door, then the camera can follow the actor with continuous medium shot. If the shot is going to be a long take, such as a student walking down the hall, then it is a good idea to use a dolly. A dolly is a platform on wheels that holds the tripod. It can be pushed around without the camera jiggling. The dolly can also be used to smoothly tape a static subject by moving around it.

Combination Shots

Some takes will require a combination of these camera techniques. A take might start with a close-up on the actor sitting in a chair, then zoom back to a medium shot, and follow the actor as he moves to the door. This is all done in one take, and as you can well imagine, it must be rehearsed. Rehearsal is not just for the actors. The camera operator should rehearse each scene to be taped until he knows exactly what is required and how to do it.

Focusing

Almost all cameras are equipped with an automatic focus. This will adjust the lens to focus according to the distance of the image from the camera. Unfortunately if an object comes between the camera and the desired image, the camera will automatically focus on that object, and the desired image will fall out of focus. The lens is continually adjusting in the automatic focus mode, so you never know when your shot will be ruined.

The safest and most efficient method of focusing is to focus the camera manually on the desired object and leave it there. There is a technique of dissolving in and out of a shot similar to the fade technique that can be done with the manual focus. You can begin the shot out of focus and slowly bring it into focus, or end the shot by slowly bringing it out of focus. This can be a very dramatic effect when used properly, and can suggest a time lapse, a dream sequence, or a flashback.

The Fade

Many cameras are equipped with a fade capability that will give you effects similar to the manual focus technique. Generally, when you push the fade button, it takes three seconds from the beginning of the fade to the complete fade out, and, conversely, three seconds to fade back in.

Various Types of Shots

Here are a few basic shots that the beginning camera operator and director should become familiar with (script cues are in parentheses):

 **Close-Up** (CU) is a tight shot on the object. If the object is a person, it is generally on the head and shoulders.

Extreme Close-Up (ECU) is a thight view of a detail of an image such as the eye.

 **Medium Shot** (MS) is a shot of a person from the wiast up.

Wide Shot (WS) is enough distance between the camera and the image to show the entire figure. This is sometimes called a Long Shot or a Cover Shot.

 **Group Shot** (GS) is a shot of a group of people.

Over The Shoulder Shot is a shot with one person's back to the camera and another person seen facing the camera over the first person's shoulder.

 One Shot is a shot of one person.

Two Shot is a shot of two people.

Two Cameras or One?

If you have the equipment, you can shoot a scene from different angles with more than one camera all at the same time. Then when you edit the scene you can break it up from various angles, giving the audience a more interesting visual experience. For instance, if you are taping a conversation between two people, you have little or no action. It is a static scene, and if it is shot entirely from one angle, it can be tedious and boring.

In a professional shooting of such a scene, generally three cameras are used: one camera with a medium two shot, and the other two with close-ups on each of the actors. Sometimes there are cameras with over-the-shoulder shots. The editor can then cut from one type of shot to another during the conversation to keep it varied and interesting.

All of this, of course, can be done with just one camera. The only difference is that when you are using multiple cameras, you can tape the whole scene in one take. When you are using only one camera, you use shorter takes and change the camera angle with each take. If you are working with inexperienced actors, this can be an advantage because the actors have shorter segments of the scene to learn at a time. Using one camera may take a little more time, but the effect is the same as using multiple cameras.

At times you will find that the actors are having a difficult time getting through a scene smoothly. No matter how many takes, they either forget their lines or get the giggles. You realize that you can use the part of the take before the actors lose it, so you cut and begin another take at the trouble point. This is a legitimate thing to do and can solve a lot of your problems. But unless you move the camera angle every time you stop and start again, the image will jump and look peculiar. The reason is that no matter how careful your actors are to stay on their mark and maintain the same position that they had in the first take, there will be some shifting of position when the next take begins. Have the students watch how those long conversations are filmed on the afternoon soap operas, and this should give them an idea of how to shoot such a scene.

The great advantage of the camera over the live stage is that you can shift location, time, and audience's point of view in a split second. This is done with creative camera work. The person operating the camera is as important as the person directing the project. And, in fact, everyone who has anything to do with producing a video project would have a basic knowledge of the camera and its operation.

Care of the Equipment

A firm control over the equipment and its care is essential, or you might find yourself out of business. Replacements and repairs are expensive, and most teachers have to deal with a mountain of red tape to keep the equipment in working order. The time it takes to get replacements or repairs may often cancel out your plans to go into a video project for the rest of the academic year. So it is definitely to your benefit to take care of the equipment and keep it in working order for as long as you can.

Most schools will have video equipment under the control of a librarian and store it in a locked room with other audio-visual equipment. Generally the teacher would be required to check out the equipment on a daily basis, and check it back in on the same day. This is a good security system, but its drawback is that the teacher has to reserve and check-out the equipment every day.

If you have your own equipment in your classroom, or if you can check out equipment for an extended period of time, then you need somewhere to store the equipment when it is not in use. A closet or a cabinet that can be locked will serve this purpose. The students must be responsible for returning the equipment to its proper place at the end of the period. Some teachers feel that it is necessary to have the students sign the equipment in and out. More equipment has been lost because it has been left lying around.

While the students are being trained to operate the

equipment, they should also be trained in the proper care of the equipment. Cameras are delicate instruments and should be treated gently. To keep the lens clean and safe from being scratched, you should keep the lens cover on when the camera is not in use.

Batteries for camcorders need special care. Make sure you read the operating instructions in the owner's manual carefully before you recharge the batteries. With some batteries, improper charging can limit their use. Also, dropping a battery on the floor can ruin the battery forever.

Tripods, no matter how sturdy, can be ruined with improper use. With most tripods you have the capability to move the camera either vertically or laterally, or there will be screw locks to hold the camera firmly in one position. If, however, you fail to loosen the screw locks and move the camera, you can strip the screw locks and ruin the tripod.

Try to keep the cameras and editing equipment free from dust and moisture. It is a good idea to have routinely scheduled cleaning sessions to maintain the equipment.

If you keep a close inventory on your equipment, and institute careful storage and care, you can prolong the life of the equipment significantly.

Tape Control

One of the most aggravating and time consuming problems in working with video in the classroom is searching for a specific tape that is not labeled. If you are convinced that video products are valuable teaching tools and you use them frequently in your classes, you will find video cassettes beginning to mount up. This can cause problems.

The solution is not solved by cramming as much as possible on one tape. In fact it is a better idea to use one tape exclusively for the takes of one project. That will save you time finding the take that you want when you are editing. It is also a good idea to have sound effects and music on a special tape in case you want to use them again on another project. It will save you time searching through an hour-long tape to find a five-second sound effect.

With the tape containing the raw takes, the sound

tapes, the master edit, and a back-up copy, you will have four tapes for one project. Then, of course, students will want copies. It doesn't take many projects to have your classroom cluttered with a lot of tapes including demonstration tapes that you have copied from commercial television for classroom use.

The first step in avoiding this kind of chaos is to label each tape religiously. Write the name of the project on the label and the tape's classification, for example: "The Seance—Master Copy." This will allow you to find the tapes quickly when they are filed.

All tapes should be kept in their jackets for protection, and within the jacket should be a complete index of what is on the tape. You can create the index as you are actually taping or write it down afterwards. The best way to keep track of the shots is to number the takes, by the use of the "slate" or "clapper." You write the name of the project, the scene, and the take number on the slate and hold it in front of the camera, and then announce orally for the audio, "The Seance. Scene four. Take two."

The students love to use this device because it's just like Hollywood. You can buy a slate with a clapper, or have some enterprising student make one and write the information on the slate with chalk or washable marker. The same job can be done by merely holding a piece of paper with the information on it in front of the camera.

Note each take on your index, and keep it in the tape sleeve with the tape for as long as you plan to keep the tape. Then you can easily find the shot that you want when you run through the tape. For more efficiency, each tape should be rewound when you finish working with it for the day.

Tapes can be stored and filed in a small bookcase. The students should be trained to always return the tapes that they are using to the case where they are stored.

The master tape of each project should be kept in a locked cabinet or in some other secure storage place. I make this suggestion because it has been my experience that master tapes have a habit of disappearing. If you follow these tape control suggestions it will save you a lot of frustration.

Chapter 4
Sound Effects and Special Effects

Creating sound effects is a small but important part of television production. The collecting of sound effects on an audio tape can be an interesting and creative project in itself. I recall a student who was failing everything and was on the brink of dropping out of school altogether. He found that this was something that he could do well, and it was instrumental in turning his attitude around. The class even created projects around his sound effects.

A humorous vignette is the project called "All Aboard!" The scene opens in the library. Students straggle in and begin to study at tables. A voice-off begins to announce: "All aboard for Biology, Algebra, English Literature, World History, and all points east. All aboard!" Then there is the sound of a locomotive getting up steam and starting off slowly, followed by the sound of a train clicking along with an occasional whistle. After a while a man dressed as a conductor enters and says, "Tickets, please." He wanders through the tables punching tickets that the students present. This project is, perhaps, a little bizarre, but it displays a good deal of imagination on the part of the students in creating a scene developed by a sound effect.

Most of the time you will be concerned with creating sound effects to fit the action of the scenes you are producing. In a commercial about a breakfast food that was supposed to be especially crunchy, the students had a problem underlining the crunchiness of the cereal while the actor was eating it. Many things were tried, but they finally settled on the sound of aluminum foil being crumpled. It was an unforgettable effect.

The sources of sound are everywhere, and collecting sounds can be a creative challenge for your students.

Special Effects

Unless you have a system that gives you a large selection of automatic effects, you will have to create them with what you have. Some effects can be done with nothing but the manipulation of the camera. Unusual camera angles or strange, extreme close-ups can produce some interesting effects. Jiggling the camera, for example, can give the effect of an earthquake or an explosion.

Some effects can be produced by lighting. We once filmed a ghost by placing a sheer curtain in front of the ghost and bathing it in a pale green light. Holding a strong flashlight under the chin can give a bizarre and sinister effect, too.

It is possible to create some effects with poster board and paint. In one episode where the actor was supposed to be knocked unconscious, we used a typical animation sequence to express this. We pained a series of pictures of stars. In each picture the stars increased in size and elaboration. Then we taped the pictures in sequence and edited them in a progression of one second each. The effect was an explosion of stars.

It is easy to make things appear as if by magic. This is done by cutting the scene, and then introducing the object that is supposed to appear. The Fairy Godmother can change Cinderella from a scullery maid to a beautiful lady with the wave of her wand using this technique.

Special effects can be fun and add to the effectiveness of your projects.

PART II
Video Projects

Chapter 5
First Video Projects

Like everything else that a teacher wants to introduce in the classroom, performance-based video projects require a certain amount of preparation to be successful. Simply pointing the camera at a student and dramatically shouting "action" will usually yield only nonsense, giggles, or deep silence. Some of the problems that should be addressed in the initial video project are the student's self-consciousness, equipment operation, voice projection, and photographic composition. The first project, then, should be designed as a kind of training run for the students (and perhaps the teacher, too).

"It Gives Me Great Pleasure to Introduce ..."
The introduction is a simple project that meets these requirements. I arrange the class in pairs and give them 10 minutes to question their partners. I try as best I can to keep from pairing old buddies with each other. This not only spreads out the concept of teamwork but can save a lot of time lost in the giggles.

The idea is that each student in the pair will introduce the other. The 10 minutes gives them time to figure out what they are going to say about each other. I allow them to take notes to which they can refer when they are on camera. It is a good idea to allow the students who are being introduced to give their partners an idea of how they would like to be introduced.

Here are some questions that can elicit this information and, at the same time, reinforce the student's self-image:

What are your main interests?

What do you like to do for entertainment?

What have you done lately that you are proud of?

What would you like people to know about you?

What would you like to have your name associated with?

At this point it might be a good idea to give the students a few hints on deportment. If the student is speaking to the television audience, he must look at the camera. Physical attitude and posture can either enhance or detract from the over all effect. The student should avoid gestures that might distract the audience, such as gum chewing, foot tapping, fidgeting, fiddling with fingers, scratching, etc. And, most important of all, the student must speak clearly, distinctly, and loudly enough to allow the microphone to record the presentation satisfactorily.

The next thing to do is to set up the camera and arrange the set. In this project the set is just a couple of chairs in front of a plain background. It is best to keep the background simple, because too much clutter will distract from the focus of the project. Make sure that the background is not too white or too bright. A window with daylight coming through or a bright white wall will turn the performers into dark silhouettes.

This is a good opportunity for students to acquire experience in operating the equipment. Each pair will operate the camera in turns as others are performing. The camera operator will focus on the speakers, making sure that the frame is filled satisfactorily with no heads cut off, etc. It is a good idea to use a tripod for the camera to make clean, steady shots.

The camera team controls the taping. One member of the team will operate the camera, and the other will direct:

Director: Ready? (This is said to the performers.) Quiet on the set! Roll it.

Camera Operator: Rolling. (Operator hits the record button.)

Director: Action! (This is the signal for the performers to begin.)

Director: Cut! (This is said at the end of the taping, and the camera operator turns off the record button.)

After all of the introductions have been taped, the project can be viewed for evaluation. This is perhaps the most significant phase of the project. The success of future video projects might very well depend on what happens during the evaluation. Handled incorrectly, a student's self-image may be damaged, or the student may be turned off the project from that day forward. Therefore, it is absolutely imperative that only positive reinforcement is voiced in the evaluation.

I usually require each student to make some comment about each introduction ... and it must be a positive comment! With this method, all the students receive positive reinforcement, and all the students have seen themselves successfully performing on the television screen.

There will be great temptation to point out to a student that he or she shouldn't have done this, or it would have been better if he or she had done that, but at this stage what is needed is confidence. The students are not stupid, and they will see what is good—what everyone mentions as good—and learn from that.

The tape is ready to be edited, which simply entails cutting out all the false starts where the performers collapsed in giggles, etc. (These false starts could be saved and included in a tape of out-takes later. This is always fun.)

The students now have a basic knowledge of what it takes to produce a video project and are ready to try something more creative. The finished first project can be filed for viewing at a later date when the students can enjoy watching their first attempts at video production.

Chapter 6
The Television Commercial

Everyone is aware of the enormous impact that television commercials have. We know of their power and the dangers inherent in the control and manipulation they have over the minds of the public. We say that we hate them and that we only suffer watching them because it is their presence that pays for the television programming that we want to watch. We use the commercial time to go to the refrigerator or the bathroom. But what we don't realize is how much we love them.

While I was in the Air Force and stationed overseas, I made an informal survey of the troops in my outfit. Each man was to list in priority order the three things he missed the most from home. Number one was unanimous: the hamburger. (The majority said "Big Mac," which in itself attests to the power of the commercial.) Number three was scattered and showed no pattern at all. I wasn't surprised at these results, but I was stunned to learn the second most-missed thing from home was the television commercial.

When the Superbowl was broadcast on the armed forces TV, we had to stay up until three in the morning to watch it because of the time differences. The military, forbidden to endorse a product from the private sector, would push a button whenever a commercial was about to be aired, and we would see some announcement about the joys of re-enlisting. It was quite a disappointment because we came to realize that part of the pleasure of watching the game on television was seeing those wonderful beer commercials. Occasionally the finger on the button would be a split second late, and we would get a flash of a commercial, and the guys would all cheer.

I was brought up in an earlier generation without television, but the radio commercials are still dear to me, and, after all these years, I still know many of them by heart. It comes to the same thing except that television commercials are perhaps more vivid because you can actually see them. These days when I accuse someone of loving their TV commercials, they usually get angry, look at me as if I were crazy, and deny it vociferously. They won't realize that what they are watching now will become the irretrievable past in the golden haze of nostalgia.

As a teacher, I am aware of not only the importance that media has to my students, but also the responsibility that I have in educating them as sophisticated consumers of the daily media barrage to which they are subject. I use video projects in my classroom as a major teaching method, and one of the students' favorite projects is the commercial. I have found that this kind of student production requires a complete spectrum of language arts skills which makes it an ideal project in an English class.

The secondary students initially will deny any affection for commercials just as the adults do, but when you begin to discuss the subject in the class, and list their favorite commercials on the chalkboard, you will find the list getting longer and longer. The students will have a great deal to say about what they like and about the elements in a commercial that make it interesting.

Commercial Gimmicks

I make a video tape collection of commercials recorded during daytime television, prime time, and during the Saturday morning cartoons, and the class makes a detailed study of them. They discover that most commercials are only 30 seconds long. It seems almost impossible that so much can be crammed into such a short period of time. But time is money in television programming, and commercial space is expensive. During the 1993 Superbowl game, one national commercial spot cost around $900,000. In practical classroom terms, the 30 second television spot is both good and bad. Such a short project is manageable to produce, but the students find it nearly impossible to get their message across in that amount of time. I usually allow them up to a minute and a half.

Then we try to determine the audience to which the

commercial is directed. The commercials adjacent to Saturday morning cartoons are obviously directed toward children. But it is possible to be even more specific by age and gender. A certain doll, for example, may have features that are not appropriate for girls of five or under. We see that the commercials in daytime television are directed almost exclusively to women; music videos show favor to teen-agers; sporting events favor men, etc. When studying the commercial, the questions to ask are who would buy the product being advertised and what techniques are used to reach that particular audience.

It is in this area of video sales techniques that the students have the most valuable learning experiences as knowledgeable consumers. Critically reading the messages of the advertisers, identifying the sub-texts, and recognizing the ticks of this kind of advertising are definitely skills that need to be addressed in the schools.

If you mention to the students that no one drinks the beer in a beer commercial, they don't believe it. But after watching a few of these commercials, they are amazed to find that it is true. This is a classic example of how the commercial producers can manipulate through the power of suggestion. Because of a kind of censorship on the product, they can't show beer being consumed, but they do an almost magical job of making you see it and experience it in the mind's eye. In this manner they defeat the thrust and purpose of the censorship.

Food always looks more delicious when it is advertised. What you actually get in a typical frozen dinner looks different than the wonderful full-course meal in the commercial. Clothes always look smart and fashionable on the anorexic models, and most products can be made to look more beautiful, larger, and more efficient on television than they are in real life.

The fallacy of "expert testimonials" can be a great discovery for the young student who has always believed that "if it wasn't true, they couldn't say it on TV." It is a simple matter to point out how statistics can be manipulated to arrive at the "nine out of ten doctors" endorsement. There is also the expert by association. "My husband is a pediatrician" suggests validity. And then there is the notorious, "I'm not a doctor, but I play one on TV." Famous people such as movie stars or sports figures add the element of glamour to their endorsements without the least bit of validating expertise. It is a good idea to keep a file on FCC rulings concerning false advertising. Such examples will show the student what some advertisers are trying to get away with.

Television commercials are expert at creating their own markets. The trick is to make the viewer believe that the product is absolutely essential to the viewer's existence. You don't realize that you really need it until you see it on TV. The example that I like to use in the classroom is the case of underarm deodorant. I point out that in the '40s, when I grew up, few men used underarm deodorant; in fact, it was considered sissy for a man to put this perfumed stuff on his body. (You can imagine the reaction I get from the students when I say this: "Eeoooo! Gross!") But the commercials won, and now everyone is afraid to raise their hand without it.

Advertising Techniques

The advertising technique that affects my students most is what I call the "in crowd" commercial. Adolescents can be very sensitive, self-conscious, and insecure. These commercials suggest that if you use the product being advertised, you will become popular and accepted by your peers. This technique has great success with many teenagers. The classic example of this kind of commercial is the Dr Pepper campaign in recent years. The question, "Wouldn't you like to be a Pepper, too?" has been directed at two generations of teen-agers, as if drinking that particular soft drink would be their golden invitation to join the "in crowd" and pass through the door to social success.

The use of sex, repetition, and even annoying bad taste aimed at getting the viewer's attention is easily identifiable. I find myself a sucker for kittens, puppies, and babies. (I don't pay much attention to the products being advertised, but I suppose their message gets to me subliminally.) Humor is widely and effectively used to get the viewer to watch a commercial. It is my opinion that some of the best (and perhaps the most insidious) commercials use humor as their sales technique.

Although I have stressed the negative aspects of the television commercial, it makes a wonderful video project. After understanding the nature of the commercial, the students are ready to start planning their own production. They are divided into groups, and each group brainstorms ideas for their specific project. The teacher may assign the products to be advertised, or leave it up to students. I always preferred such products as disposable underwear to reduce laundry or edible pencils for that pre-lunch snack.

I require the groups to identify the specific audience and decide on the sales technique that will be appropriate for their product. Then they write the script and compose a production sheet for their project. The production sheet will include the names of the director, technical personnel, actors, the location, props and sets, and a shooting schedule. I usually require them to create a story-board which is like a comic book with a panel for each camera change. This will give the students a visual idea of what they want the video to look like.

With some help and direction, they will be able to shoot their project in two or three class hours. Editing can take another couple of class hours depending on the sophistication of your editing equipment. In this phase you can add music, a voice-over, or other sound effects. I would like to emphasize, however, that satisfactory projects can be made with only a video camera, a VCR, and a television set.

The students will love it and want to look at it over and over. To complete the impact of this learning experience on the students, they must know that others have seen the project. It is absolutely necessary that the teacher find some way of publishing the projects, either to other classes, PTA meetings, closed-circuit television, etc.

An analysis of the skills required for such a project will justify the classroom time it takes to complete one: two weeks classroom work (or more), for 30 seconds of product. But the students are exercising analysis, writing, organization, speaking, leadership, and creative skills along with assimilating music, art, and pictorial composition. Few other projects can do so much. The students have created one of these wonderful little visual dramas, and may even have experienced an introduction to a possible career choice. But what is perhaps even more important, they have become sophisticated critics of the television commercial that is wielding so much power in today's society.

•

Chapter 7
Producing the Drama

The Curse of the Mummy

The project that is dearest to my heart is the video drama, probably because it is such a versatile project which can be adapted to most of the elements that I am trying to teach, and because there are a variety of ways the project can be approached.

Adapting Literature for Video Production.

Students can select a short story or an episode from a novel being studied in the class and adapt it for video. Some of the things that you need to consider when you are writing the script are the limitations of your shooting locations and set, the casting, and the cinematic techniques used to deal with time lapses and scene changes. In other words, you need to make sure that the production is feasible, considering what you have to work with.

If you have a small number of students as actors, then you need to select a story that you will be able to cast. If the story takes place in a life boat on the high seas, you are going to have to figure out how that can be accomplished or select something else. But don't give up too easily. With the imagination and ingenuity of your students, it is possible to come up with some very interesting and exciting effects and techniques that will allow you to produce shows that at first might look impossible. My class produced a story about a murder in a fun house at a carnival. With some sound effects, a few props and Halloween masks, and a lot of darkness, we taped the entire story in one corner of my classroom.

The Monkey's Paw

One project that seemed particularly suited for video production was "The Monkey's Paw." This famous story is included in almost every English curriculum in the country at one level or another. It has a small cast—two women and three men—and most of the scenes take place in the parlor of a house. The dialogue and action were easily adapted to a shooting script.

With little difficulty we arranged the parlor set in a corner of the classroom, and had some fun creating the actual monkey's paw. The entire production turned out to be fairly simple until we got to the climax of the story where the son, who has risen from a horrible death, returns to the house. Then we really had some fun experimenting with make-up, sound effects, lighting, and interesting camera angles. The actor playing the son limped, crawled, groped for almost an hour as we experimented with the camera. We edited it together and had plenty of interesting shots to illustrate the action dramatically and effectively.

The possibilities of adapting literature to video productions are virtually unlimited. It is as appropriate in kindergarten as it is in high school. The video project is a way to make the literature come alive and be meaningful to the student in areas that just can't be reached with merely reading and discussing.

Videos from Original Compositions

Some creative writing assignments can naturally progress into video projects. Students' original short stories, whether they are ingeniously plotted or simply a slice of life, can be the starting point for successful video productions. It is a special challenge for the writer who will soon learn that additional dialogue has to be written for exposition, and that descriptive passages are quite useless in a video script. You may, if you like, begin with teaching video scripting as a writing or composition experience.

The Curse of the Mummy

One of the most successful dramas produced by my students was "The Curse of the Mummy." I like to have all my classroom projects generated from the literature that is studied in the class. We had been studying ancient literature, which included some ancient Egyptian poetry.

The students tried their hand at writing similar poetry. Then we researched Egyptian phonetic symbols and translated the poems into hieroglyphics.

One of the students brought in a video cassette of one of the many early films with the theme of the mummy's curse. We enjoyed the film and decided that we would make our own, but we needed to know more about the subject. There were 16 students in the class, which we divided into eight research pairs. Each pair researched one aspect of our topic: The Dynasties of the Pharaohs, the tombs, mummification and the Egyptian belief in the soul's travels after death, the discovery of King Tut's tomb, stylization in Egyptian painting, etc.

When the research was completed, we conducted a seminar in which each pair shared its research with the group. Then we made a biographical history of our mummy, and took particular note of the research information that we would need to write our script, build our set, and manufacture our props.

A team of four students went to work writing the script. After a number of false starts, including one opening scene with three Arab excavators who appeared to have escaped from a Three Stooges movie, the beginnings of a working script was produced. Throughout the taping there were changes made in the script as new ideas presented themselves. A number of endings were being considered right up to the time for taping the ending scenes. At first I felt a little uneasy about this, believing that it was a weakness in the organization of the production; but when I realized that such great films as "Casablanca" had the same problem, I rationalized that we were in good company.

While this was going on, another team of about five students was busy building and painting the set. Most of the play took place in the tomb, and so the set people spent a lot of time painting hieroglyphics and stylized figures of the pharaoh and other deities on the corrugated cardboard walls. The rest of the students tried their hands at copying pictures of Egyptian artifacts with cardboard, papier-maché, and paint. (More details about set building and props will be addressed in another chapter.)

When script, set, and props were all prepared it was time to begin the taping. Decisions had to be made as to who would play what roles. There were five roles for males, and only one role for a female. We cast it as best we could with the people that we had. You never know who is going to turn out to be a good actor in your class; in fact, you may not have any students with much talent in that respect. But you do the best you can and the results will be satisfactory, and sometimes spectacular. There was a girl in that particular class who, besides being quite attractive, had been studying dance for a number of years and was very talented. We created a part for her as the goddess Isis who appeared undulating to Middle Eastern music at the beginning and at other specific points in the play. The effect was unforgettable. The archeologists discovered the tomb and the curse, everyone died off at regular intervals, the mummy made its gruesome appearance because its tomb was disturbed, and at last it rested in peace in its cardboard sarcophagus.

The pattern of this project can be used with almost any research problem. Often the research can be as rewarding and as interesting as the video itself. The students seem to be more enthusiastic about doing library research when they know that it is gong to be used for something other than merely writing a boring paper about some ancient stuff.

Chapter 8
The Soap Opera

From the very beginning I thought that the soap opera would be the vehicle with which we could accomplish some of the things we had set out to do when we started our video program. The soap opera has one positive value that the other projects do not have: it gives the students the opportunity to explore and act out social, family, and personal problems. Heaven knows that the students of today, whether they be of elementary age or adolescent, are beset with an entire spectrum of serious and destructive problems. This can help the student understand his or her problems, if not actually solve them. It also gives the students a chance to add some humor into their projects and to act out roles that interest them.

The soap opera format is well known. There are about three story lines going at the same time; they are produced in episodes, and each episode ends with a cliff-hanger; and most of the story is carried by dialogue. Because of the multiple story-line, it is easy to cast all the students in the class, and everyone will have a chance to participate as an actor.

The most realistic setting for a student-produced soap opera is the school campus. Since the cast is all students, it is not so much of a stretch for them to play the roles of students. Many of the students' social problems are centered on the school, and for some students, school is the problem. Finally, you have a tailor-made filming location. Most of the action will take place in the classrooms, hallways, cafeteria, etc.

The initial brainstorming session would include listing all of the characters and characteristics that the students would like to see in the project. Much of the success of the project can hinge on this. If they don't find the characters interesting, the project will be almost meaningless to them, and what is more, no one else will want to watch it either.

I usually get a list that would include the conceited girl, the football hero, the gang leader, the girl with the alcoholic mother, etc. It is a good idea to give the characters names right away. That makes it easy to identify the characters and to keep everything straight when you are developing the story lines.

I always allow the students to select the roles that they want to play at this point. Some conflicts may arise, but the students usually work that out themselves. When each student is assigned a role, he or she buys into that character and becomes concerned with the way it is portrayed. From the acting point of view, the student actors are already developing characteristics which will make their performances more realistic.

The next step is to outline the first episode: what will happen first, next, and so on. Finding a place to start can be traumatic. When all else fails, I suggest the beginning of "Grease." It is the first day of school in the fall, and a new girl arrives who has transferred from another school. After that, anything can happen. (She can't find her classroom and gets help from a guy with a jealous girlfriend. Boy meets girl, and we're off.)

After the outline is done, the script must be written. I usually assign the students who are going to have dialogue in an individual scene to write that scene. You may often find that you have a couple of students who are born script-writers, and they can help everyone.

It is a good idea to try to shoot the scenes in sequence as far as possible. You can use the original outline as a shooting schedule, checking off the scenes that have already been shot, and planning the scenes for the next shoot.

Costumes are generally not a problem because, for the most part, the costumes will be what the students wear to school everyday. One costume problem, however, always exists, and that is the problem of continuity. If the actor enters the scene in a green sweater, and ends the scene in a pink blouse, the audience will notice it right away, and it can ruin the scene. This makes following the schedule important. If the actor comes to school in the wrong clothes you can't shoot the scene, and you could lose a day of shooting. Generally, I try to get the students to bring the costumes that they are supposed to wear in the scene and leave them at the school until the scene is shot. Most of the students don't want to wear the same clothes two days in a row anyway.

Aside from the various locations on the school campus, other specific set requirements may arise. That is where the little classroom studio comes into play. Most interior sets can be suggested with a little creativity, from a hospital room, to a parlor, to a bedroom.

You will find that the other students in the school will become interested in the program if they get a chance to see it. The ideal situation is to have a closed-circuit TV system on the campus, such as Channel One, and to broadcast the episodes throughout the school during a homeroom period. You could schedule showings for specific classes or departments. It is sometimes possible to show the episodes during lunch in the cafeteria. Whatever the method, the participants must have the opportunity to show their work to the student body, or much of the purpose for the project is lost.

If the suspense is handled properly, and cliff hangers end each episode, the audience will become eager to see each successive episode. The actors will find that they have become famous on the campus, and they will be besieged to give away hints as to future developments in the story line.

The number of episodes will be up to the individual class depending on the amount of time the class has to devote to the project. But the project will be well worth the trouble. It is a rare class that will not identify the soap opera project as their favorite project of the school year.

Chapter 9
The Documentary

One of the more practical and useful forms of video production is the documentary. Television programming is filled with documentaries on almost every conceivable topic. In reality, a television documentary is an informative essay with moving pictures added, giving it another communication dimension, and thereby making it more effective.

The students must select the subject for their project just as they would select a topic for a research paper, but the topic must be something that has a visual impact. They must limit the topic to ensure the clear focus of the composition, and to make sure that there are research sources available. The questions that the students must answer are: Are there library sources available on the topic? Are there subjects for interviewing available? Will the students be able to obtain enough video to cover the subject satisfactorily?

One of the best methods for approaching the production of the documentary is to have the students write the essay just as they would write any other research project. This may require considerable research in the library or information received from experts. They must, however, bear in mind the video possibilities of the material that is included in their essay. This would apply to topics such as historical sites or events, scientific or political developments, or social phenomena.

A very simple way to make a documentary without actual video sources available, is to video tape still pictures to illustrate your commentary. You have more than just a slide show because you can intersperse the video of the commentator with the still pictures. This is especially useful for essays on art, historical or current events, and historical personalities.

The essay is only a draft and will probably have to be altered after the video is finished, but it will probably remain basically intact. It will give the project form, and it will provide material for voice-over commentary when it comes time to edit.

Of course some topics need little if any of that kind of research. One of the best student documentaries that I have seen was on the subject of shoes. The thesis was that people's personalities are often reflected in the shoes that they wear, and that perhaps something can be discovered about the society by a study of its footwear. The production group spent a lot of time roaming the campus and recording people's feet with a video camera.

This is good, original research. When the group had exhausted the number of different types of shoes that they could get on video tape, they went about the business of studying the material that they had collected and classifying the shoes. There were a number of interesting observations that could be made about the people who wore the shoes, and about the group as a whole.

Then it was time to write the essay based on these observations, and from the essay a voice-over script was developed. This then would guide the editing, giving the students an idea of how to select what material to use, and in what sequence.

I find this kind of project extremely useful and creative for the students. It requires that they look closer at the world in which they live, and make observations of details that they have taken for granted. As an English teacher I am constantly trying to urge my students to use concrete imagery in their writing. This is what you do with a video camera. The students soon discover that the small visually concrete images on the television screen are the things that are the most interesting in the production.

Here are some suggestions for this type of video research that might be fun:
- The students' lockers: their condition and how they are decorated.
- Pictures and mottoes on tee shirts.
- Types of notebooks.
- Decorations on notebooks.
- The food in the cafeteria.

• What girls carry in their purses.
• Hair styles.
• Fashion.

There are any number of topics for original video research that can be done on the school campus. The topics can cross the curriculum. The students develop their research skills; they learn how to observe aesthetically, intelligently, and creatively; and they exercise their ability to organize. This provides much more learning experience than the simple research report.

Chapter 10
The Television News

Television has had a profound effect on the way news is presented to the public since the days when the news was decimated by newspapers and radio. With television you have live motion pictures of the news making most descriptive works superfluous because the audience can see what is happening for themselves. Television news has fallen under some justifiable criticism because it is suspected that if the news is not accompanied by an exciting video bite, it doesn't get reported. On the other hand, news that otherwise might not be worth reporting, is broadcast to the world because there is good video action.

As with any news media, the way the news is presented can bias the impression the news gives. For instance, all candidates for high political office seem to complain that the news media is being unfair to them regardless of their political affiliation. But the positive aspects of television news reporting seem to outweigh the negative. The audience becomes more personally involved with the news and understands it more completely when the event can actually be seen as it happens.

With discussion and an elementary study of television news, the students can be made aware of both the positive and the negative aspects of this medium. I think it is of great importance for the students to be able to watch the news and make intelligent judgments on what they see. Having the experience of preparing a news show will give them a first hand knowledge of what it takes to produce a news show and what its limitations are.

Types of News Shows Produced in the Classroom

The main problem with which you have to deal is the problem of presentation. Are you going to try to broadcast on a daily basis, weekly, or monthly ... how often? It will depend on how much time you must have for other things.

The Daily News Broadcast

If you want to do a daily broadcast, then you must keep it small. Some classes have one or two "Anchor People" read the school announcements daily. Even with a production as simple as this (and visually uninteresting), it would take nearly a complete class period to prepare it for each day, and there wouldn't be time for anything else. On the other hand, the beauty of this kind of production is that it is relatively simple to put together, and you can rotate the students who are featured to give the reports on a daily basis, thereby giving everyone a chance to participate and be seen.

It is probably better to tape the presentation than to give it "live." That will give you the ability to correct errors and avoid technical mishaps. To have a daily broadcast, you would have to write, set up, rehearse, tape and edit on a daily basis. If you have time for that kind of preparation and feel that you want to devote your entire class to it, then you might want to consider this type of project.

The Weekly Project

Presenting a broadcast of the news once a week will give you time to make a better production. This will allow you to send cameras and reporters out for specific stories. Your production can include live video action and interviews.

If your broadcast is on Monday, then you can start at the beginning of the week covering important assignments, organize and shoot anchors on Thursday, and edit on Friday ready for presentation. As you can see, even with a week to prepare, you still will have little time for anything else. It is, however, a good deal better than trying to broadcast on a daily basis. It requires more creative video, writing, and organization, and the students will have a more complete learning experience.

The Extended News Roundup

Most teachers, as it is in the case of my classes, do not have the kind of classroom time to devote to regular and current news broadcasts. But the news format can still be used in more extended news roundups. A monthly news roundup or a news roundup at the end of each grading period is still valuable for the students. (On my campus there are six week grading periods, and I find this an ideal sequence for the news format.)

The audience appeal of these newscasts is high because the students who make up the audience will get an opportunity to see themselves on TV. This is something to bear in mind when you are producing your show. It is the same principle as the old newspaperman's advice to print as many names as possible on a story (and spell them right), because people like to see their names in the paper.

Organizing the Newscast

When you are organizing the newscast, one of the main concerns will be what you are going to report and how you are going to report it. A professional television news studio will generally have various categories such as local news, national news, international news, sports, weather, and human interest or feature stories.

Some school newscasts which are oriented to current events and social studies will follow the same patterns and use the same categories as the professional news. However, I have found that it is better to focus on campus news or any news that has a direct bearing on the students of the school. With this limitation, the video and news gathering sources are fresh, original, and of more immediate interest.

The Assignment Chart

It will be necessary to collect a list of projected news events whenever you can. Club events, class events, sports events, projected changes or visits are some of the things you can plan for. All the students in your class can help make up the list of things that you want to report.

An assignment chart is helpful in organizing this kind of news coverage. On the chart you can list the events, the dates and locations, and who will be responsible to video tape and report. The chart should be permanently posted and updated when necessary so the students will be able to know what they are required to do and when they must do it.

The students can be assigned "beats" as it is done with newspapers. The various categories of news can be divided up to make sure of the coverage. Some students will want to cover sports or some other category in which they might have a personal interest.

Covering a Story

At least two students would be needed as a reporting group to cover a story. One student is needed to do the camera work, and another is needed for interview or commentary. The team should do as much research as possible before taping the story, so that the students who make up the team will have some idea of what they want on their video and have some intelligent background for the commentary.

The team must decide if there is something visual that can be recorded for the story. With a sporting event you have the actual event that you can tape as the visual basis for your story. If the drama club is rehearsing a play, some footage of the rehearsal can serve this purpose. Many of the most news-worthy stories will have good visual video opportunities like these, and your commentary often can be a simple voice over. However, an introduction as well as concluding remarks by the reporter is much more effective. The reporter should be video taped on the location of the story to give the production more immediacy.

Sometimes an interview can make the story more effective. Often the interview is the only thing the reporter has if there is no visual action associated with the story. But with a little imagination, the reporter and camera operator can dream up some visual action to help the story. For example, if the news item is an announcement of a change in the lunch schedule, a short interview with the person in charge of the cafeteria is appropriate but not very visually interesting. The story can be given added interest by showing students going through the lunch line and eating. This video can be used during the introduction and conclusion of the story.

Of course some news stories cannot be planned in advance. These are stories that pop up from nowhere, and they are often the best stories in the news cast. The students have to be ready to be on the spot with camera and notebook as quickly as possible.

Putting It Together

After all the news stories have been gathered, each story should be edited individually. This is the time that the editors decide what footage to use and where to use voice-overs. Judgment should be used to make sure that the stories are not too long. The stories should be pertinent and to the point. It is a good idea to edit the individual stories as soon as possible, so that most of the work has already been done when it is time for the final edit.

Once all of the stories are edited to your satisfaction, the decision must be made as to the order of the stories. The anchor team then must write its commentaries. It is advisable to have two or three anchors to give the presentation more variety, but it is possible to use just one.

A program logo can be created to be shown at the very beginning of the broadcast accompanied by some specific music or sound effect by which the broadcast is associated. The anchors are then shown, and the show is introduced.

The anchor(s) will introduce each story and the reporters, and conclude the broadcast. With ongoing preparation of the anchor's comments, the whole thing can be taped in one day.

The newscast is a valuable learning tool that can be as simple or as elaborate as you care to make it. It has a practical immediacy that will be appreciated by the entire school body and the faculty as well.

Example of an Assignment Chart

ASSIGNMENT CHART
Feb. 22 to April 14

DATE	EVENT	Time	Camera	Reporter	Wrap	Edit
25 Feb	Basketball Game	7:00	Alvarado	Gomez	3 Mar	5 Mar
4 Mar	Duke Dance (Interview contestents and follow up)	7:30	Bellows	Perez	25 Feb	28 Feb
1 Mar	Baseball Tryouts	3:30	Alvarado	Gomez	28 Mar	2 Apr
12 Mar	Academic Meet	to 3:30	Williams	Ramirez	15 Mar	
28 Mar	Science Olympics	3 days	Williams	Ramirez		
10 Apr	ROTC Awards	2:30	Ayala	Winslow		

Chapter 11
The Music Video

MTV has had a profound effect on the American teenager with regard to television media. For generations teenagers have called popular music their own. They have identified with this music, and they have frequently required the music to identify with them. With the advent of the music video in more recent years, the visual requisite of these presentations has equaled if not completely surpassed that of the music itself. It is the video that will sell the music in most cases.

It is not surprising, then, to find that the students are generally eager to try a music video if they are given the chance. But once they have launched into the production, they may find that it is not as easy as they imagined.

The music video takes as much planning as any other project, and there is more to it than a bunch of kids dancing to the music. The first decision that you have to make of course is which music will be appropriate for your project. Hand in hand with that decision will be deciding which approach the visual part of your project will take.

There appears to be three basic visual forms to the music video. First, there is the performance video. In its simplest form it is just a moving picture of the artists performing the music. Then there is the video that tells in pantomime a story that is suggested by the music. And, finally, there is the montage of images, sometimes almost surreal and often visually poetic, from themes suggested by the music. Many music videos combine these three forms. More often than not, the students will decide on the music because they can visualize the video rather than try to adapt the method to some specific recording.

The Performance Video
When the students decide to do a performance video, the idea is to dress up like the musicians and pretend to play the music on the sound track. This can be a lot of fun

for the student who can work out treasured fantasies of being a rock star. They can put on the outrageous "Kiss" make-up and cavort with guitars with traditional rock and roll posturing.

One of the main problems with this kind of video is that it can be monotonous and uninteresting. The costumes and make-up can help a lot, but it is varied camera angles that can make all the difference. How these shots are arranged and synchronized with the music will take a good deal of creative energy.

Lip-syncing is another technique used in these videos. This is where the actor pretends to sing mouthing the words in pantomime with the singing on the sound track. There can, however, be a big problem with lip-syncing in synchronizing the video with the audio. Editing this kind of material requires exactitude and can be very frustrating.

Of the three major forms of music video production, the performance video, which seems at first to be the easiest, is, in fact, the most difficult to produce. But often the results can justify the aggravation of these presentations. I have in mind three young men dressed as three grotesque Supremes and lip-syncing "Stop in the Name of Love" with body movements, hand gestures, and all. This video was the comic highlight of my class one year, and I drag it out to show successive classes as an example of what can be done.

Another format that is fun to try is the kind of thing done with the famous "We Are the World" music video. In that video a large group of well-known singers contribute individually and in ensemble to the production. As a class project, the students can get a number of campus personalities to lip-sync parts of the number. Members of the faculty who are secure with their own dignity can usually be coerced into contributing, and you will have something that will be interesting to try and that the entire school will enjoy.

The Music Video that Tells a Story

If you want to avoid the problem of synchronizing lips with sound and the problem of making essentially static scenes interesting, you can try the music video that tells a story. In this technique, you simply videotape action in a story suggested by the lyrics of the song and fit the video sequentially to the audio.

Take, for example, a song about lost love. (I am sure, of course, that you will not be surprised to find that there are many, many songs about lost love.) The lyrics suggest that the singer has lost his lover to someone else; he recalls how wonderful it was when they were together; he feels that he can't go on without her; and so on. The video scenario can go something like this:

- The boy is looking dejectedly at a photograph of the girl. He begins to daydream. (Fade)
- (Fade in) The boy and girl are walking hand in hand down the school hallway.
- (Cut to) The couple is sitting under a tree, his head in her lap.
- (Cut to) The couple is in the library doing their homework together.
- (Cut to) The girl is playing a trick on the boy in good fun. (Fade)
- (Fade in) The boy looking at the photograph. (Fade)
- (Fade in) The boy and girl having an argument, and the girl leaving angrily. (Fade)
- (Fade in) The boy looking at the photograph. (Fade)
- (Fade in) The boy is standing there watching the girl walk down the hall hand in hand with another boy. (Fade)
- (Fade in) All he has left is the photograph.
- (Fade to black.)

As you can see, the scenario is comparatively simple to write and fun to shoot. With a little good planning a video such as this can be produced in a fairly short amount of time. It is ideal for a class that has only a very limited time for such a project.

The Montage

Creating a montage as a visual response to the music

is similar to creating a collage on a theme where you cut out pictures from magazines and paste them onto a base. This technique can allow the student to take flights of creative fancy by using concrete imagery. As all English teachers know, teaching the use of concrete imagery in writing prose and poetry is perhaps the most elusive and difficult skill to put across. But students seem to understand it naturally when they are dealing with visual images.

The making of a collage with pictures and paste is a good pre-production activity. Also, a study of surrealistic art would be a good preparation for this project. A collage is, by its very nature, surreal in that you are juxtaposing images without regard to natural context or perspective. With these experiences under the student's belt, he or she will feel more comfortable in working with this most poetic medium.

Some Technical Problems

If your equipment does not allow you to dub sound (audio) without affecting the picture (video), then you are practically confined to do the music video in one take while the music is playing. This is because you must have a continuous and uninterrupted sound track of the music. This would be very difficult to do, and it severely limits the video options that you have.

Fortunately, most VCRs allow for the kind of dubbing that is needed for this kind of production. You should tape the music first, continuously from beginning to end. Then you can fit the video images to the music later. It is almost impossible to do it the other way around, because the music must be uninterrupted.

One of the many positive things about the music video is that you don't have to worry about the quality of the sound. If the quality of the audio recording that you are using is good, then the sound quality of the video will be good, and all you will have to concern yourself with will be the quality of the visual images.

The music video is an appropriate project for any class level from K through 12. Even difficult students, who aggressively attempt to avoid participation in classroom activities, can be seduced into project involvement by the music video. The teacher who detests hard rock and rap as musical forms, may end up loving them as vehicles to obtaining student involvement.

Chapter 12
Video Vignettes

To most of the average students in secondary schools these days, classical music is something that is very dull, can put you to sleep, and should be avoided at all costs. Teachers of humanities have tried to overcome this prejudice by requiring the students to listen to the music and discuss or write about the images that the music inspires. Unfortunately, this teaching strategy has very limited success. But using classical music as a basis for a video vignette can help the student appreciate the great expressive possibilities of this music. The student will be selecting appropriate music and actually working with the music apart from merely listening and trying to visualize.

It is not especially necessary to select program music for this project because almost any music will do. Let the students know that they are looking for background music for their videos; play a number of musical selections for them; and let their imaginations go to work. Sometimes it is best for the teacher to select and assign the music that the students will use, but it might be a good idea to play a variety of different compositions, and allow each team to select the music for its own individual project.

The students are aware of much more classical music than they realize because they hear it constantly in films, animated cartoons, and commercials. When you play selections from Mozart or Beethoven, they will frequently respond with, "Hey, I've heard that before." This identification with something familiar in the music will go a long way in breaking the students' prejudices, and perhaps will be the beginning of a list of classical music that they like.

Because of the practical limitations, only a three or four minute section of most musical compositions could be used. After the teams have made their selections, it is a good idea to provide each team with an audio cassette recorder and a tape of the music. This will help them visualize their ideas, and they will want to play the music over and over when they are trying to outline their video.

Creating a story board is essential with this project because the students are developing the visual out of existing audio material. It will be necessary for the students to find specific places in the music to cut from one shot to another. The best way to identify the location of a particular shot within the music is by using the counter on the audio cassette recorder. The count number can be noted on each story board frame to facilitate the editing.

An example of this kind of musical vignette which was produced in one of my classes was made with a section from the scherzo of *A Midsummer Night's Dream* by Mendelsohn. The music suggested someone running helter-skelter, and this idea led to a scenario of a student who is trying to make it to class before the bell rings. The opening shot was a girl hurrying down the walk to the school carrying a large stack of notebooks and texts. She struggles to open the door, and in her panic she drops a book. Once inside, she runs down the hall, up the stairs, and collides with someone coming the other way. Her stack of books is scattered. Her panic grows as she gathers the books up, and just as she is about to open the door of the classroom, the music ends and the bell rings.

This kind of project is relatively easy to produce if you can keep the content simple. Try to direct the students to limit the action and focus on one emotion or idea that will fit into this small format.

Students who are ardently interested in sports can use videos of basketball, football, baseball, etc., as the video base for a vignette used with classical music. Ballet music is appropriate music as a background for sports, because the movement and grace required on the playing field is similar to the movement of the ballet dancer. The students will probably be familiar with this type of vignette, because it is very popular and is frequently used professionally in conjunction with sports broadcasts.

Landscapes, nature, scenes of city activity, or pictorial

studies of buildings, monuments, or neighborhoods could make interesting vignettes with only music as the sound track. The key to making such a vignette successful is finding the appropriate music to fit the video, taping interesting and varied pictures, and editing the pictures creatively.

These small projects are often used within a larger production. They are frequently included in a documentary film to illustrate some specific location or idea, or enhance a presentation that otherwise would be dry and uninteresting.

Using Poetry with Video

Somewhat allied to finding video to fit a selection of music, is using video to illustrate poetry or poetic passages. This can be a valuable project that can be used when teaching literature. "Daffodils" by Wordsworth comes immediately to mind as a project that would work well with classical music. All you need is someone's spring garden for the video, and a student who recites well to provide the audio. In addition to this, it is an excellent way to present the students' original work.

A Montage of Still Pictures

A collection of still pictures can be taped and arranged in an interesting sequence by editing. This works especially well with a musical audio base. Photographs illustrating some major event or period in history, sports, art, etc. make interesting projects. This technique usually consists of taking shots of the still pictures for from three to five seconds. You should play the tape back after each shot to make sure that the picture is clear and in focus.

The taping is a little time consuming, but it is very versatile and can be used with many teaching units across the curriculum.

Chapter 13
The Mini-Teach

Video projects can be used in conjunction with curricular objectives regardless of the class or the grade. This can be done effectively with the mini-teach, a video project where the students reinforce an objective covered in class by creating a video and teaching it in some interesting manner. Not only will it reinforce for the entire class the objective or unit being taught, but also, the students who have participated in the video project have become experts in the skill demonstrated.

The Student Teaching

The mini-teach can be a straight-forward teaching demonstration. With this method the student takes the part of the teacher or the expert and explains and demonstrates an objective skill. This project can have at least a limited use in any class taught from the first grade through the high school.

Teaching with Commercials

The use of television commercial techniques in teaching elementary language has been successfully demonstrated by such programs as "Sesame Street" and "The Electric Company." The parts-of-speech salesman can extol the value of the multiple uses of the adverb, or the fine assortment of prepositions available. He could advise the audience to get rid of the old, weak passive voice, and try the new, improved active voice. These commercial techniques can be surprisingly effective in such courses as mathematics and science.

The Quiz Show

Teachers who frequently use the quiz show format to reinforce objectives realize the benefit of competition in promoting enthusiasm for the study. Videotaping these sessions will give the students the enjoyment and opportunity of seeing themselves performing, and at the same time the objective is being reinforced. If the teacher keeps the tape on file, it can be valuable as a vehicle for review.

The quiz show can be scripted to reinforce some particular objectives such as the identification of figures of speech. The idea is to make the project look like a professional quiz show, but everything would be created beforehand. There would be the contestants, the quiz master, and the assistants to the quiz master. The quiz master would introduce the show and the contestants. A passage of poetry would be read, and the contestant would attempt to identify the figure of speech that it illustrated. After the contestant's answer, the definition of the figure of speech would be read, and the show would progress until someone won the contest.

Though this method takes more preparation, the students will bring more creativity to the project and have more control over the production. This video project can be used to reinforce knowledge of any classroom subject.

Historical Dramatizations

Dramatizing events in history is, naturally, especially suited to social studies, but historical dramatizations can be used in other classes where historical events play a significant part in the subject. A dramatization of Fleming's discovery of penicillin, or Thoreau going to jail, are every bit as appropriate as a dramatization of the signing of the Declaration of Independence.

The research for this project can be considerable, and its value alone can justify its use. The procedures outlined in the chapter entitled "Producing the Drama" would apply with this project.

The Mock Trial

A trial has strong inherent drama, and the dramatic possibilities of the courtroom have not been lost on playwrights and television producers. You will find it a very versatile teaching strategy, and the students will most certainly display enthusiasm for this project.

An example is a trial to judge Tom Walker, from the

story "The Devil and Tom Walker" by Washington Irving. Everyone in the class can participate including the camera crew, the lawyers, the judge, the defendant, the witnesses, and the jury. The source of all testimony must come from the text of the story.

Considerable preparation is necessary for the project to be successful. The team of lawyers both for the prosecution and for the defense must prepare their cases, and select and prepare the witness for cross examination. Some knowledge of courtroom procedure will be necessary. The students will probably need some firm direction or chaos can prevail.

The Debate

Closely allied to the mock trial is the debate. Within almost any subject taught, there will be many points that can be debated. The students must be prepared beforehand with the knowledge of debate argument and rebuttal procedure. And of course they must prepare their cases. The debate can be scored by the class in general.

I like to assign a number of short debates in order to involve as many students as possible. It is easy to find questions for debate in literature, for example: Should Huck Finn in the book by Mark Twain be allowed to continue on unsupervised and uneducated even though he is only 14 years old? In *Great Expectations* by Dickens, was Magwich solely responsible for his actions, or was he a victim of society?

Videotaping the debates will allow the students to evaluate the performance of the participants, and when viewed later, will allow the students to further evaluate the questions being debated.

Exploring such questions encourages the students to delve deep into the substance of literature, and helps them to begin shaping their ideas and philosophies in regard to human existence.

Chapter 14
Community Service

Once your class has successfully created a video project, and it has been shown throughout the school, you and your students will probably be looked upon as experts in video production, and you will be called upon to perform various services for the school and the community. This is another aspect of working with video that can build self-image in students who need it. A request for their skill and expertise from other sources sets them apart, and they become proud of what they can do.

The administration of the school will usually come up with a number of requests for the services of your students, including video coverage of special visitors to the campus, speakers, and events. A typical project that can serve the school is a video presentation of the school and its activities. Such a project can be used as a freshman orientation film, or something to show important visitors what the school is all about. If you find that you have to "sell" your classroom program to the school administration for whatever reason (purchase of equipment, inclusion in curricula, etc.), this kind of service may be extremely helpful in convincing those in power of the value of video as a teaching vehicle.

Teachers of other courses will be calling for your service, too. My class has made video of JROTC drill competitions, science fairs, sports events, displays, and demonstrations throughout each school year. Some teachers will request the assistance of students skilled in the use of the camera to help them make their own classroom projects.

In this age of high-tech education some teachers get overwhelmed by the operation of technical equipment. Frequently I am asked "to send someone down to see if they can get the VCR working." With the experience that my students have, they can usually identify the problem quickly and set things right.

Public service organizations, other schools in your district, church groups, and local government organizations may ask for your services. A university class in architecture that was working on a project to make proposals for the improvement of a city park requested the students in my class to make video study of the park to be used in their final presentations. The project was interesting and successful, and the university presented the class with a plaque that celebrated its participation in the project. Students can gain a great deal of experience and self confidence working with projects like these. The students have the opportunity to interact with the community, and this may be the most important experience of all.

Individual family projects such as weddings, parties, and debuts can be opportunities for your students to work with their skills on and to make a little money, too. I have had a number of students who have gone into business for themselves providing these kinds of video services. A video yearbook can be an excellent fund-raiser at the end of the year.

It is easy to get swamped with these "community service" requests, so it is often necessary to set some limits as to the amount of time you will be able to spend on such services. However, with good, flexible scheduling you will find that almost everything is possible, and the rewards are great.

Frequently, students, who have been graduated from high school for some years, come to visit me and request to work on some video project of their own using our editing equipment. I am always delighted to see them, and I always make time to help them and to allow them access to the equipment. They may be doing a youth project for their church, a presentation for a college assignment, or a demonstration for some community organization. Whatever it is, it is proof that the video projects in my classroom have had positive and practical effects.

Chapter 15
Kindergarten Video

Every school level from kindergarten to 12 is an appropriate level for using video projects and finding value in them. My daughter, Teresa, is a kindergarten teacher in the Austin (Texas) Independent School District, and partly from my influence she began to do video projects with extraordinary success. This has given me an insight into the problems and techniques in working with video in the elementary schools. On a couple of occasions she sent me her raw tapes, and my high school students edited them. They loved working on these projects and exercising their expertise.

Producing a video project in kindergarten requires some different strategies than what would be used in the high school. Before the actual project begins, the teacher must use the camera frequently in the kindergarten class to let the students become accustomed to it. It is a good idea to let the children act out in front of the camera. Encourage them to make silly faces. This is fun for them, and when you play it back for them, they see themselves acing silly, and for once in their lives, they will get approval for this behavior. The teacher can show them home videos where the teacher is acting silly too. This is all they need to realize that it is okay. This will blunt the novelty of being before the camera, and get a lot of the silliness over before beginning the project when it is definitely not wanted. Mainly, these activities erase the fear and inhibitions that the students might experience in the presence of the camera.

It is advisable to wait until after spring break to start your video project. With very young children, it takes that long for the students to get into a routine and develop personal and social interaction. By spring they have learned the rules and know the boundaries between when the teacher is having fun and when the teacher is serious. In short, their behavioral expectations have already been firmly set. It also gives the teacher time to teach creative dramatics, improvisations, and pantomime well before the project begins.

Three Billy Goats Gruff

One of Teresa's most successful projects was developed from a unit that she was teaching about the farm. The students had learned the song about the Three Billy Goats Gruff, and they decided to develop a musical drama around this song.

Of course the idea is to use every student in the class as the cast of the project. They had to expand the story as it is outlined in the song to include more characters. Mother Goose made an appearance and there was an astonishing three-headed troll. A restaurant with a cook, waitress, etc., was added where the goats went to eat their grass.

The costuming was comparatively simple because most of the actors could use items from the dress-up center. Some costuming items had to be made, like the goats' horns and the garment for the three-headed troll-it was a sheet with three holes in it.

The set was also easy because of the items that had been brought into the classroom for the farm unit; for example, a bale of hay, an egg basket, stuffed farm animals, etc.

The first thing that was taped was the song being sung by the entire class, to be used both as video and as audio voice-over. Fortunately the kindergarten classes stay with their teacher the whole school day, and it took the whole day to complete this taping. Little ones need a lot of breaks and a lot of help. There were occasions when the teacher had to turn the camera on and then hide behind the students to help them with the song. The song took a number of takes.

After a shooting schedule had been developed, the taping of the play began. The song carried most of the story line as the students pantomimed the action. Some dialogue was necessary, and this was improvised and rehearsed.

Kindergarten teachers usually have no trouble obtaining volunteer parents to help out, and their services can be valuable when you are trying to produce a video. You will find that parents are eager to see their children perform on video. It will probably be necessary to shoot the individual scenes away from the class in general because of the noise and the distractions. A volunteer parent can take care of the class while this taping is done.

The teacher must model the body movement and the gestures desired for the student actors because most of the students will have no idea of what to do. The teacher needs to exaggerate the gestures and facial expressions to transmit the idea to the children.

The shooting on this particular project took two weeks; however, they taped only three days a week because it was considered necessary to break the routine and allow the students to participate in other activities for a while.

The teacher can edit the tape, or get help. If someone else is going to do the editing, it is absolutely necessary that a detailed script is provided for the editor. This will necessitate studying your tape, sequencing the takes to be edited, and indicating the use of the audio. (See section on scripting.)

Mother Goose MTV

A simpler project is the music video. Of course you will need to organize a number of them so that all the students can participate. Various types of popular music can be included in your program, such as pop, Motown, country, rap, etc.

The music can be taken from professional recordings, or live music. (My daughter and some musician friends created some of the music for her project.) If you need help, you can go to the music teacher, who will probably be delighted to assist in your project. At any rate, the first step is to tape all the music.

You can organize the casting using two to six students for each song. The students can choose the kind of music they want to work with, to a certain extent, with the teacher guiding the decisions. The teacher then works with each of the small groups. Center time when the students do independent work is ideal for these sessions.

Again, parents can be recruited to make costumes, to help as dressers getting the students ready for taping, and to supervise students that are not involved with the current shooting. Some parents have special skills that you can enlist, such as carpentry, sewing, etc.

The students can paint background scenery on butcher paper and make specific props.

After all the preparation, one music video was taped a day. Some of the students danced, some tried to lip-sync, and some pantomimed. All of the videos were taped inside except one: a Jack and Jill video was shot outside because there was an exceptional hill location on the school's campus.

The Rewards

One of the residual benefits of the video project in the elementary school is the support that it attracts. It is a tailor-made project for getting parents involved in the students' education. Anyone who has ever taught school knows how important that can be. Also, each parent is going to want a copy of the tape.

With this kind of parent response, your school's administration will take notice, and you will find that you will have more support from that sector. It might become easier to ask for equipment. It is also possible to apply for grant money from various sources for special projects such as these.

My daughter has a "gala opening" one evening after the project has been completed. Everyone is invited: administration, faculty, staff, and parents. The dress is semi-formal. Invitations (student-made) are sent. Refreshments are served. It is a big deal and wonderful stuff for future support.

This kind of project is a valuable teaching strategy for language development and self-esteem. It may provide a way for a child to get his or her parents' attention. It helps the young students understand a story more completely when they become the story. It can give meaning that might be missed when someone is reading to the student.

There has been substantial feedback from teachers who inherit the students who have had the experience of producing and performing in a video project. These teachers are pleased to find that their students are much more verbally expressive than those who have not had that opportunity. They read with more expression, and are much less inhibited in reciting before the class.

The emphasis here has been on kindergarten, but the same principles apply throughout the grade spectrum. Generally speaking, the older the children are, the more responsibility they can handle in all aspects of the production. If, for instance, you teach the sixth grade, you can develop a project somewhere between the kindergarten projects just described and the high school projects outlined in this book.

Appendix A

A Glossary of Helpful Terms

Audio: The sound part of a video recording.

Blocking: The actors' positions during the performance that have been planned and directed beforehand.

Camcorder: A video camera with a battery power source that can be used free of an electrical outlet.

Character Generator: An editing device for recording letters and numbers on the video tape.

Cliff-hanger: The technique of ending each episode in suspense in a serialized production.

Commercial: A short video advertisement.

Cut: A command to end the scene and to stop recording.

Documentary: A video essay edited in a dramatic form.

Dolly: A platform on casters which holds the tripod to enable one to move the camera about smoothly. As a script cue—dolly in, dolly out, dolly left, etc.

Edit: Organizing and assembling takes into a final product.

Extreme Close-up: A camera shot at very close range on a detail.

Fade: A camera technique that gradually fades the picture out.

Flat: A covered frame used for scenery and back-drop on the stage or TV studio.

Glitch: A distorted break in the video editing.

Group-shot: A camera shot of a group of people.

Lip-sync: Pantomiming the act of speaking or singing to a previously recorded sound track.

Location: An area away from the TV studio that is used for an environment for video taping.

Logo: A symbol used for a product, TV station, or program.

Medium Shot: A camera shot that is usually from the waist up.

Monitor: A television screen.

News Anchor: The television news presenter who introduces the show and controls the newscast.

News Beat: The news-gathering responsibility of a reporter.

One-shot: A shot of one person.

Out-take: A take that is not used in the final edit generally because of a mistake.

Pan: Rotating the camera horizontally to give a panoramic effect.

Pantomime: Action without speech in a performance.

Prime Time: The period of time when more people are watching television than any other time.

Prop: (Property) An object used in an acting performance such as a telephone or a newspaper.

PSA: A public service announcement. It is similar to a commercial but is not commercially sponsored.

Set: The scenery and area in which a scene will be shot.

Slate: (Clapper board) A board on which the scene and the take number is written. It is recorded on the tape before each scene is shot.

Special Effect: Usually a camera or editing effect that must be produced technically.

Story Board: A collection of small drawings which indicate the camera angle and the action of the video project in sequence.

Take: Each segment of a scene being shot from the time the recording begins to the end of the shot.

Tripod: A three-legged support for the camera.

VCR: Video cassette recorder.

Video: (As opposed to the audio) That part of a recording that shows the picture.

Video Cassette: A cartridge case containing the video tape which is designed for automatic insertion into the camera or VCR.

Zoom: An automatic lens adjustment allowing the camera to move steadily from a long shot to a close-up.

Appendix B

Example of a Story Board

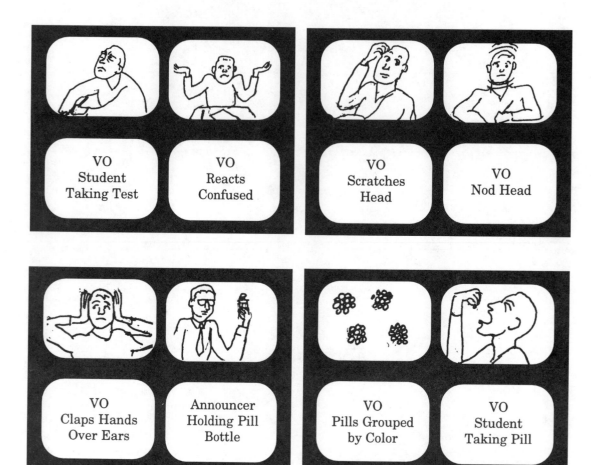

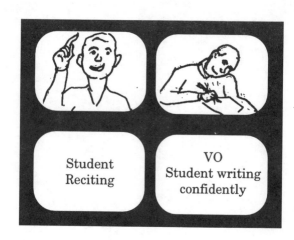

Story Board